PEEPS®

A Candy-Coated Tale

MARK MASYGA AND **MARTIN OHLIN**

ABRAMS IMAGE • NEW YORK

8 a.m.: Welcome to Peepsville, where sweet folks celebrate life's simpl

pleasures. Here is a typical family greeting the new day.

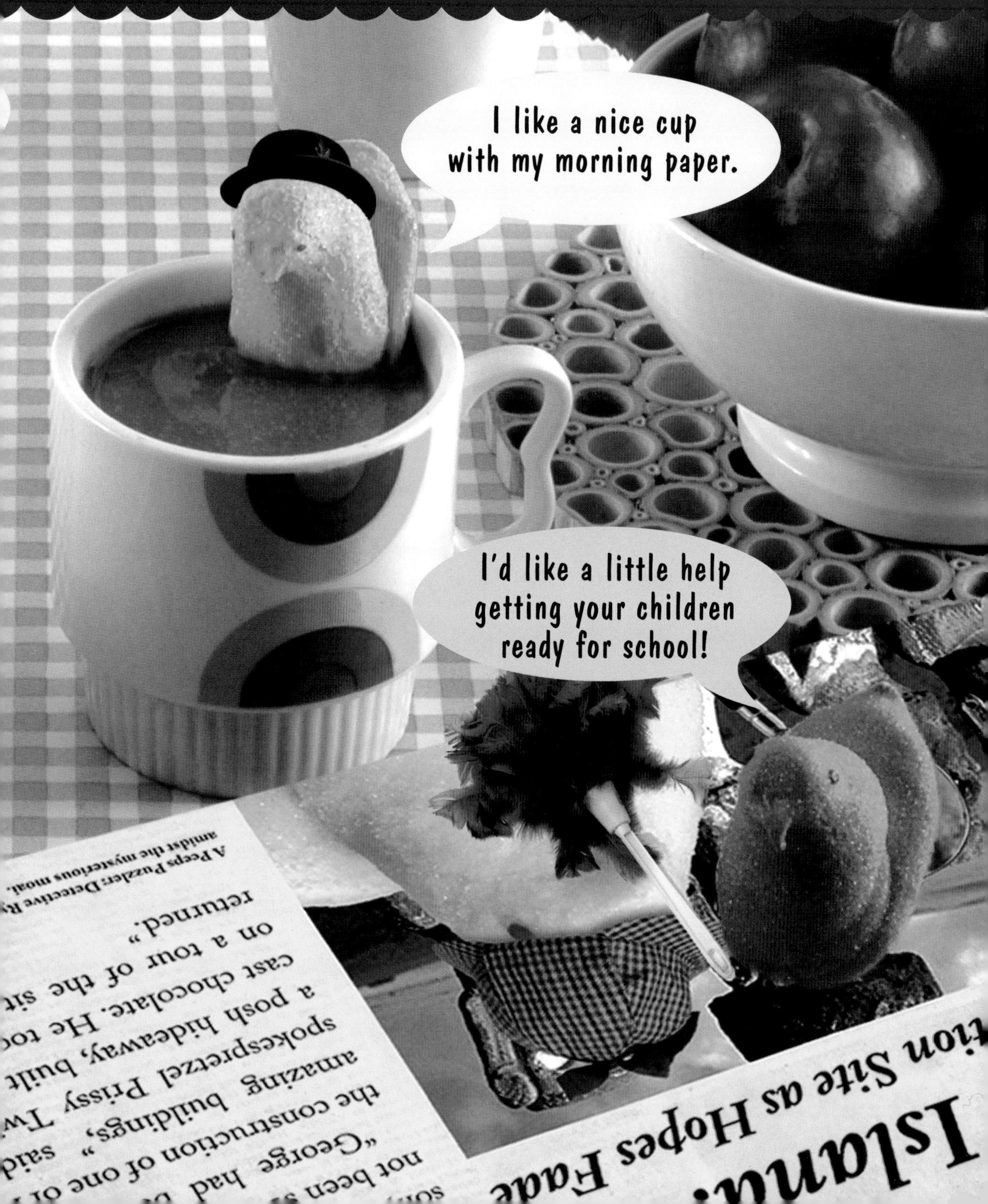

The Peeps

VOL. XXIV...NO. 33,444   PEEPSVILLE, W.

Prominent Peeps Fa
Missing on Easter

Rescue Crews Comb Construction

ville Currant

"raisin' your awareness."

ONESDAY, APRIL 5, 2006   SIXTY-TWO CENTS

mily
Island!
Site as Hopes Fade

RAPA NUI — Officials of Easter Island's Rapa Nui Resort confirm that the prominent Peeps family —architect George, 50; talk-show host Crystal, 45; their daughter, Sugar, the actress, 25; and their son, Brian, a nutritionist, 22—have not been seen since last Tuesday.

"George had been supervising the construction of one of his most amazing buildings," said family spokespretzel Prissy Twister. "It's a posh hideaway, built entirely of cast chocolate. He took his family on a tour of the site. They never returned."

A Peeps Puzzler: Detective Ryan Zachary searches for clues amidst the mysterious *moai*.

Hopes of finding the clan alive diminish with each passing hour. "It rained last night," said Detective Ryan Zachary, head of the rescue efforts. "That spells trouble for the Peeps's sugary coating. We hope they were able to find shelter among the island's craggy bluffs."

George Peeps designed many of Peepsville's most spectacular structures, including the Museum of Peeps Art.

A few days earlier on the island, Sugar Peeps completed filming the highly anticipated *Jurassic Peep* with Brad Peep and Peeper Sutherland.

Brian Peeps was reportedly supervising his celebrity sister's diet. "No one else would hire him," said Prissy Twister.

Crystal Peeps joined her family last Sunday for what she had billed to the press as a "joyful vacation of reconciliation and healing." The vacation was being filmed as a special episode of Crystal's weekly PEEPS Television talk show *Sweet Nothings*.

Some critics had decried the outing as a naked grab for ratings.

"In light of George and Crystal's widely reported bickering, most

George Peeps: Candy architect nonpareil

Crystal Peeps: Television's marshmallow mouthpiece

candies are wise enough to know when they're being played," said Professor Marsha Mallow, who heads the cultural studies department at Peepsville University. "Do George and Crystal still care for each other? Who knows? Does Crystal still care for big ratings and mass adulation? You bet! What better scheme than to hook up with her famous family on Easter Island for a sentimental televised reunion? She'll do anything to keep her name in the papers."

Detectives have interrogated members of Crystal's film crew, who were not invited to tour the construction site. "I know candies are questioning Crystal's motives," said cameraman Lester "Peanut" Chew. "But as someone who has worked with her for many years, I think this vacation was the real deal. Crystal wanted to mend her fences."

"We have very few clues to work with," said Detective Zachary. "We found a wad of chewing gum stuck to a rock, but she hadn't seen anything. On a hopeful note, a suspicious fragment of fluff turned out to be seagull droppings. Still, after three days, I fear the worst."

Brian Peeps: Ludicrous lump of goo?

Sugar Peeps: Sparkling starlet

Dominic Flees Home Confinement

Peepsville Officials Confirm Ankle Bracelet Monitors Were Chewed Loose

PEEPSVILLE — Dominic the guinea pig has broken parole and apparently fled Peepsville for parts unknown. The ankle bracelets used to monitor his whereabouts were found gnawed to bits near a stack of travel brochures and airline schedules. "We followed his droppings as far as the Peepsville International Airport," said Detective Larry "Pop" Sicle. "We believe he's traveling under an assumed name."

In 2005, Dominic was convicted of devouring Peepsville's marshmallow Christmas tree. The controversial verdict was based solely on the testimony of local celebrity Crystal Peeps. Following six months' imprisonment, the notorious rodent was sentenced to five months of home incarceration.

"I don't know why we

"Dominic is innocent," said Mandrake Peeps

ever let him out of prison," said Warden Constance Bunny. "Once those critters get a taste for marshmallow, there's no turning back. Some guinea pigs are known to have devoured up to five Peeps in one sitting."

"Dominic is innocent,"

Dominic, the former school mascot, has broken parole and disappeared.

said Mandrake Peeps, Dominic's master. "Guinea pigs don't like marshmallow. Everyone knows Crystal Peeps is a sugarcoated slanderer."

In 2000, Dominic was fired from his position as Peepsville High School mascot after PTA Board President Crystal Peeps criticized his lack of pep. "He just sits on the sidelines munching turf," she complained.

"No one actually saw Dominic eat the Christmas tree," said Mandrake Peeps. "Crystal will do anything to keep her name in the papers. I believe she paid Mike and Ike to haul the tree away in their vaudevillian surrey. Crystal needed more fodder for her stupid talk show. Keep running, Dominic! Wherever you are, I miss you, buddy."

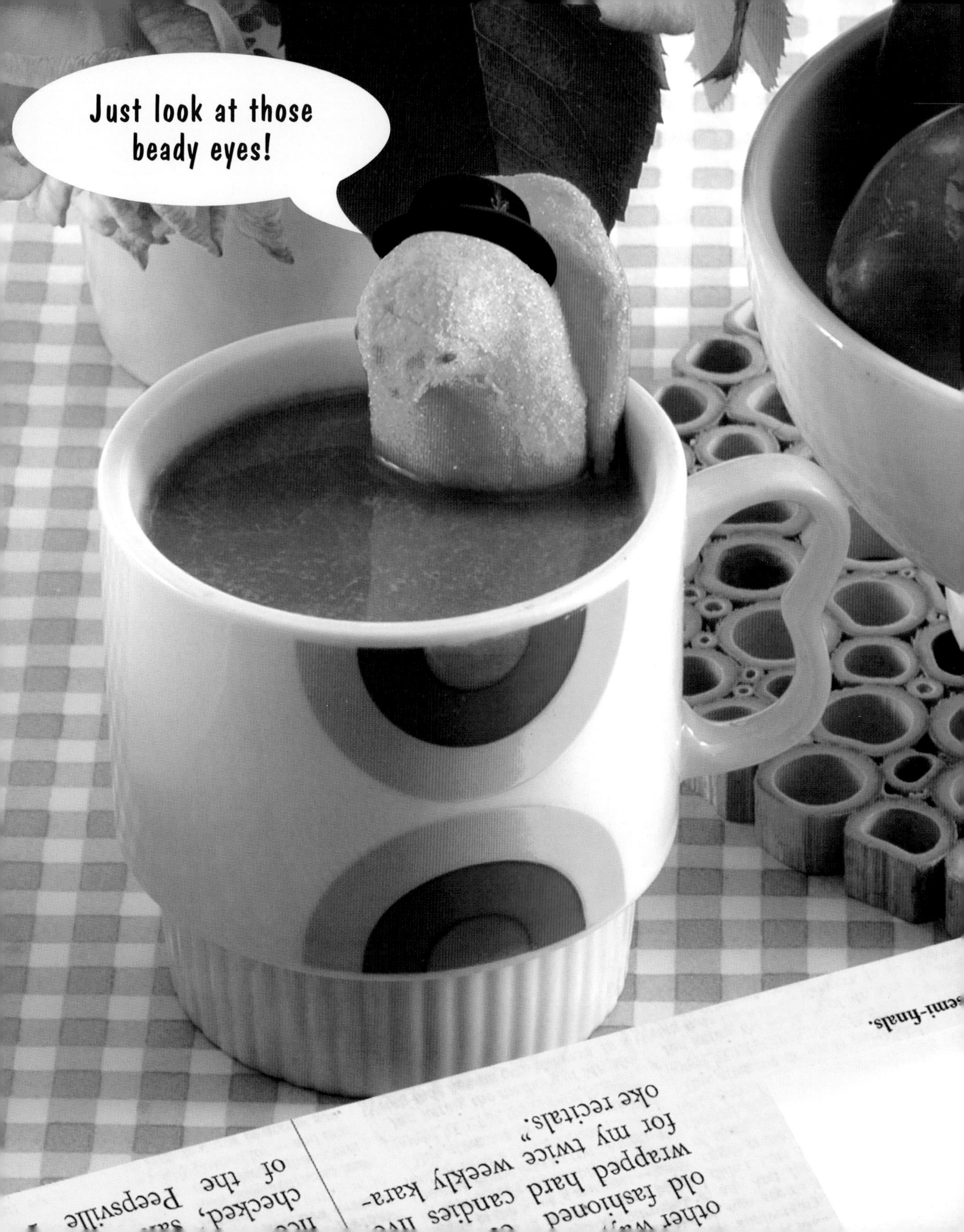
Just look at those beady eyes!

Local Candies Compete on Peep Idol

By Bibs Carnauba

PEEPSVILLE — Darla Fondant has a song in her heart and she's not ashamed to share it with the world. "I love to sing," she said. "I prefer sugary pop ballads, but I'm good at hip-hop, too. My parents agree that I'm probably the greatest candy singer of this or any previous or future generation."

Miss Fondant, a Peeps bunny who lives with her parents, Patricia and Bill, recently taped an episode of *Peep Idol*, the nationwide talent competition that airs on PEEPS Television. Fondant performed "Forever Your Goo," the 1987 hit of *Peep Idol* judge Peepla Abdul. Her performance will air on the program sometime next month. [*Spoiler Alert: If you don't want to know that Fondant loses the competition and is forcefully ejected from the sound stage, stop reading this article.*]

Fondant's performance received an overwhelmingly negative response. She was forcefully ejected from the soundstage before the final bars of her number. "Those judges were very judgmental. I think they must have had trouble hearing the mellifluous magic I was emitting. I mean, I saw Peepla Abdul plugging her big ears with cotton candy right after I started warbling. I was very hurt when they lied about my incredible talent. I think

Balancing act: Ada Peeps warbles her way into the semifinals.

they chose Ada Peeps just because she's one of those popular yellow chicks. They get all the breaks."

"Darla's singing, if you can call it that, was nothing short of horrendous," said Abdul, the singer/choreographer turned talent barometer. "She absolutely butchered my big hit. Jeez, I was so steamed, my gorgeous sugary shell started to dissolve. Ada Peeps, on the other hand, was just magical."

Ada Peeps, a senior at Peepsville High School, performed the Runyon Peep Jones hit "Tangled Up in Goo" while balancing a stack of miniature marshmallows on her rounded noggin. "Ada won fair and square," said Peepla Abdul. "She'll have a long shelf life!"

While Miss Peeps will proceed to the semifinals, Darla Fondant will continue to pursue her musical dreams. "My fans at the Crystal Dish Retirement Facility wouldn't have it any other way," she said. "Those old-fashioned cellophane-wrapped hard candies live for my twice-weekly karaoke recitals."

Recent "Peepsquatch" Sighting Chills Spooky Cat

PEEPSVILLE — Higgly Piggly Jones might be a Peeps Spooky Cat, but she never thought of herself as a *scaredy* cat until she encountered the Peepsquatch.

"Call me crazy, but I know what I witnessed," said the seasonal favorite. "I was chasing a Teenee Beanee down a back alley when I saw the elusive creature rummaging through a Dumpster. I was petrified! He must have been at least three inches tall, and he was covered from head to toe in rich white frosting."

Jones found refuge behind a garbage can. "Luckily, the Peepsquatch hadn't seen me. I watched him devour some discarded sugar. He seemed very hungry, actually."

Local officials quickly dismissed Jones's story. "No one wants to disparage a Halloween favorite, but we think Higgly Piggly Jones needs to have her eyes checked," said Billy Bunny of the Peepsville Police Department. "The Peep-

squatch is an urban myth. Frankly, we don't have time for such nonsense."

Frosted Frightener: Was this photo fudged?

PEEPSVILLE CINEMA CLASSICS

20,000 PEEPS UNDER THE SEA	7:10, 4:13, 9:90
CROUCHING PEEP, HIDDEN MEANING	4:11, 2:22, 11:59
THE ADVENTURES OF PEEPSILLA, QUEEN OF THE DESSERT	1:01, 19:13, 4:07
ERIN PEEPOVICH	0:19, 3:33, 11:07
THE PEEPER CHASE	7:10, 4:13, 9:90
ROBO PEEP, PART I	7:10, 4:13, 9:90
PEEPER MOON	9:60, 4:02, 13:00

New Peepsville High Principal Has Worldly Vision

PEEPSVILLE — Oliver Sugarman has lived and worked all over the globe, from his birthplace in rural Candyana to Fudgistan and beyond.

"Everywhere I go, I visit the schools," he said. "Anyway, that's what I told those Board of Education folks. Luckily, they're a bunch of suckers."

Last week, the Peepsville Board of Education hired Sugarman to replace Brick Halvah as principal of Peepsville High School. "He's an excellent choice," said Schools Superintendent Lolly Jo Pop. "Mr. Sugarman appreciates the basics of any solid candy school curriculum, from marshmallow extruding to sugar spinning. But he's also aware that in today's changing world, our kids have to be prepared for new challenges. We were particularly excited by his plans for foreign chocolate

Sugarman (far right) with the school board

studies, apple dipping, and licorice twisting. We're a bunch of suckers and Mr. Sugarman easily persuaded us that he's the best candy for the job."

A twist of fate brought Mr. Sugarman to Peepsville in 1998. "My elderly parents were getting stale. I checked

"They're a bunch of suckers."— Oliver Sugarman

them into the Crystal Dish Retirement Facility and met an enchanting young candy striper named Ginger Breadman. It was love at first sight. We were married soon after."

Sugarman spent eight years sitting around his wife's cramped apartment before landing his interview with the Board of Education. "I needed to build up my strength after all that traveling. Plus, they've got some excellent programs on PEEPS Television."

Cricket Star Accused of Assault

CORAL GABLES, FLORIDA — Semiprofessional cricket forward Hobart "Sam Dunk" Peeps was charged Wednesday with assault of a 19-year-old sponge cake at a Brighton resort, where the victim worked.

"After looking at all the evidence, I can prove this case beyond a reasonable doubt," said Edwin Lipscomb Sticket III, attorney for the Brighton forward. The 25-year-old Brighton Limping Flagons star, who has a 2-year-old chicklet, was charged with 3 counts of assault, a felony. If convicted, Mr. Peeps faces a sentence of 20 years to life on probation, and he will lose custody of his custard-filled child.

The charge also carries a fine of up to 750 pounds. "I'm definitely innocent," Mr. Peeps said at a press conference Sunday while vacationing in a Coral Gables, Florida, strip mall. With his mother and attorney at his side, Peeps paused to dab syrup from his

Hobart "Sam Dunk" Peeps

cheek and said quietly, "Gosh, I didn't force her into anything. All I did was wheech a purler down the track and pitch it straight to her. I mean, look at the replay." Mr. Peeps issued virtually the same statement earlier in the day when he signed autographs, but added, "Last week I had 3 singles and no balls, and you guys never blinked once."

The dessert cake alleges she was a victim of Mr. Peeps's advances at the Brighton resort where she works. The following day she filed a complaint with Bobby, a local bobby. No details of the victim's allegations have been

made public, and a local judge has sealed any information related to the case. According to Ewan McNaugahyde, custodian at Roquefort Hills Resort, Mr. Peeps stayed at the hideaway the weekend of the alleged misconduct.

Brighton officials issued an arrest warrant for Mr. Peeps, who gave no resistance and was released on bond. "It is alleged that Mr. Peeps made unwanted advances toward the sponge cake, using physical force and his beak to caress her golden crust," Mr. McNaugahyde told reporters. Eagle Territon, Britain's cricket commisioner, issued a statement later in the weekend: "As with all allegations of criminal nature to baked sweets, this makes me ill. It makes me want to smash a four through the onside and then nick another with a fine edge. On the way home from the pub last night I faced an antisweet tirade hurled in my direction by a fan. It isn't fair."

TV LISTINGS

SWEET NOTHINGS – *talk*
What do you do if a coworker approaches you at the water cooler and says he's sweet on you? Self-help author and Golden Pretzel Award winner Polly Sorbate, 80, knows how to differentiate between innocent office flirtation and saccharine sycophancy. Host Crystal Peeps helps cut through the fluff.

CIRCUS OF THE SWEETS – *variety*
In this episode of the TV classic, Brooke Shields and Nell Carter race overweight turtles (force-fed on chocolate turtles) across a bed of broken, molten, flaming glass; Peepscilla Presley dangles by her teeth over a pot of chocolate fondue; Barbi Benton roller-skates under a platform holding 200 wooden audience members, through a wall of flaming wax lips, and into a bystander reading a bus schedule; Carol Channing drinks too many lattes and begins eating things off the top of a nearby orangutan's head, startling him; and, in the finale sequence, Willie Aames and Charlene Tilton exchange pleasantries and toiletries while riding a tandem unicycle around an undulating mound of nougat.

THE PEEPER CHASE – *very old school*
Spun off from the movie of the same flavor, a bottom-feeding student, James T. Fennimore Hart (Timothy Bottoms), must make a choice between making the grade or making out with a cute chick in law school. Things heat up when he realizes she just happens to be the nubile daughter of one Professor Charcoal Kingsford III (John Outhouseman), Mr. Hart's contract bridge teacher. It's fodder for father, who always knows best, at least for 13 episodes.

Word Search!

```
F B R W L T C E E T J T P I N J
O Q S N R M G S S P D N O T Y L
R R Y Q A A T O Y T U S T B I O
E A I U G C O Y R V R C A I R R
S B W I U A Y N U T A W S T S E
H T A N S R R N P T R U S E S S
A T T T P N I G T C A V I T Y U
D N I U I A O Q C U E E U O R U
O S A P I U S A R R P A M L U S
W P X L R B T I N G E E S C P A
R E G E L A T I N I E F O I L T
C W M T T W L N S N P T R U A E
C R Y S T A L T J U S T B O R N
N T Y U Y X B A R E S C A T S P
L O C S R S H T C R A F T S O R
O R T C T R E P E R A O E T E B
Y S J R T A R L L A N B A P U L
E N U A D R L L Y E A R B O O K
J B A P S P I D R T S O R A O P
A E I B U T O H I D E A W A Y C
I I T O A I E S U S C S T T T N
L G I O B W A M B N H N T C D E
E E U K A C H O C O L A S E R O
R I G S E R T T S L L S A B S P
S A I L O B S T R E P E R O U S
```

sugar

carnauba wax

crystal

potassium sorbate

gelatin

obstreperous

crystal dish

hideaway

cavity

Peeps

quintuplets

crafts

Just Born

beige

syrup

scrapbook

foreshadow

yearbook

chocolaser

Local Authorities Debate Authenticity of Horrible Scrapbook

PEEPSVILLE — A local Peeps chick, custodian Mandrake Peeps, discovered a horrifying scrapbook while mopping the private quarters of Dr. Rosebud Roberts, Peepsville's first human resident and the director of the Marshmallow Treat Foundation. "Man, that scary book gave me a jolt!" said the janitor. "I saw a picture of my friend Deborah Johnson glued to a wooden picture frame. I called the police right away."

Detective Billy Bunny of the Peepsville Police Depart-ment describes the find as "a frightening document. It's a scrapbook, full of crafts and recipes which submit Peeps to numerous injustices and indignities."

"The scrapbook is obviously fake," said Dr. Rosebud Roberts. "I don't know how it got placed on my crafting table, but anyone can see that these cruel images were Photoshopped together. No one would really make crafts out of you nice candies. Trust me! Humans want to be your friends. And they would never eat you. That's just ridiculous."

"We shouldn't let humans live in our candy community," said Hazel Dugan, a cellophane-wrapped hard candy. "I've nestled in my share of candy dishes, and when people come calling, sweets tend to vanish."

Other candies scoff at Dugan's warnings. "I believe Dr. Rosebud Roberts," said Schools Superintendent Lolly Jo Pop. "All of us suckers believe her. She's ethical and trustworthy. It's a shame someone would try to frame the good doctor by embossing her initials on the scrapbook's cover."

Dr. Roberts was briefly questioned but no charges were filed. "This case is still under investigation," said Detective Bunny: "Any concerned Peeps who would like to judge the book's authenticity are invited to stop by police headquarters and take a look. But be forewarned: It's not a pretty sight. Whether or not those photographs are authentic, I'm *still* losing sleep."

Detective Bunny invites Peepsville residents to inspect the terrifying tome.

Peepsquatch Frosted Treat

Ingredients:
Marshmallow Peeps® Bunny

White frosting

Red icing

Directions:
Frost a Marshmallow Peeps® Bunny on all sides. Don't be afraid to glop it on!

Add some red icing eyes.

What a strange and mysterious creature you've created! Are you brave enough to eat him?

School Memories Picture Frame

Ingredients:
Marshmallow Peeps® Chicks, Bunnies, Eggs, etc.
Plain wood picture frame
Acrylic paints
Paint brush
Tacky glue

Directions:
Paint the sides of the picture frame in your school colors. If your school didn't have any official colors, beige is a safe bet. Good luck mixing beige, though.

Glue Marshmallow Peeps® candy around the frame. Wait! Is the paint completely dry? Come on, folks, we can't make it much easier than this.

Insert a gorgeous photo of your sweetest school chum. Or frame your own portrait and give it to a friend.

Poor Deborah Johnson always wanted to be in pictures...

...and there she is, <u>on</u> pictures!

Piggyback Snack

Ingredients:

Graham crackers

Chocolate bar

Marshmallow Peeps® Bunnies

Those Peeps have retired in style!

Directions:

A graham cracker lies face down. The chocolate bar climbs on the graham cracker's back. Two Marshmallow Peeps® bunnies plop on top of the chocolate bar. They won't listen? Well, you'll have to help them. Once you've got everyone settled, take them for a spin in the microwave. It should only take a few seconds, depending on your appliance. Delicious!

Crystal Dish Centerpiece

Materials:

Crystal candy dish. If you don't have a crystal dish, any clear dish or bowl will work.

Aged Marshmallow Peeps® Chicks, Bunnies, Spooky Cats, etc.

Just Born Jelly Beans

Directions:

Make sure your crystal dish is very clean. Do you have a feather duster? Use it!

Add the Just Born® Jelly Beans. Try not to eat too many—these are for decoration!

Gently place the aged Marshmallow Peeps® Chicks on top of the jelly beans. Be careful! Some of these folks might be a bit brittle.

Invite other candy friends in for a lovely visit.

Now you have a spectacular centerpiece to enjoy year-round.

Peepstock Fudge-In

Ingredients:

Marshmallow Peeps® Bunnies, Chicks

Brownie mix

Chocolate frosting

Directions:

Bake the brownies in a 9-by-13 inch pan. Or use a different size, baby. Whatever feels good!

Let the brownies cool before frosting. Smear a little chocolate frosting on some Chicks and Bunnies so it looks like they've been dancing around in a very muddy field. That's beautiful!

Arrange the Peeps haphazardly on top of the brownie.

My kid could do that!

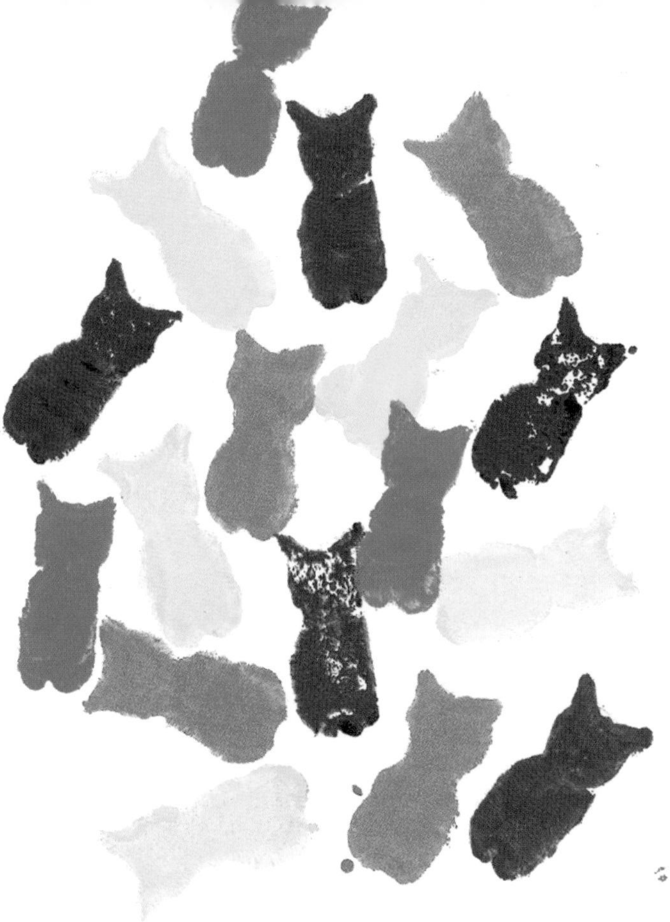

Cocoa Cat Prints

Ingredients:

Marshmallow Peeps® Cocoa Cats

Tempera or acrylic paints

Paintbrush

Paper

Directions:

Paint the front of a Cocoa Cat. Use your imagination! This is supposed to be fun.

Press the Cocoa Cat onto the paper. No, the painted side, silly! Don't push too hard.

Look! It's a Cocoa Cat print! Why not make a design or spell out your name?

Peepsville Residents Suffer Heat Exhaustion
Tragedy Forestalled by Alert Hard Candy

Hazel Dugan, hero.

PEEPSVILLE — Tragedy was averted yesterday when a trespassing hard candy alerted authorities to a sticky mess on Lollipop Lane. The mishap occurred at the home of Vern and Laeticia Bunny, who were practicing yoga poses with Graham Cracker and Choco Barr in the backyard.

"Graham is awfully stiff," said Barr, by telephone from the Peepsville Clinic. "We tried to help him articulate some basic poses by jumping on his back. No one noticed that the sun had risen directly overhead. Well, we halted our half-baked efforts when Vern and Laeticia's sugary bums had sunk a good quarter inch into my rich chocolatey goodness."

"It was a life-altering experience," said Vern Bunny. "We were merging into a crazy group consciousness. We started singing campfire songs while Graham told spine-tingling ghost stories."

Rescue workers received a call from Hazel Dugan, a cellophane-wrapped hard candy. "My granddaughter is a gum ball, so she keeps me rolling around like crazy. I had no choice but to follow her into the Bunnys' backyard.

"At first I thought I was witnessing a lewd event," said the old-fashioned sour drop. "My wrapper was crinkling with indignation. It was s'more than my heart could take. I was shielding my granddaughter's eyes when I realized these unfortunate folks were actually suffering from heat exhaustion."

Emergency workers removed the party en masse to the refrigeration unit at the Peepsville Clinic, where they are expected to make full recoveries. "Of course, some disfigurement is to be expected," said Dr. Jennifer Corduroy. "But it's nothing a little high-fructose corn syrup can't fix."

That's warm!
Daddy's gooey!
I'll tell them you'll be late for work again, honey!

PEEPSVILLE
HIGH SCHOOL

WELCOME
SWEETS
OR SOURS

10:30 a.m.: No one is too old for show and tell! Porky's friend Pegg
to Jon Lipzowacks, who is Brian Peeps's second cousin onc

Dang!
How do we open it?

To:
a smart peep HaHaHa
I met a long time ago
oKillian Kornsyrup "02"

TO Brian,
I feel the chicks
Were across the sea,
What a good swimmer
you would be.

from,
Ahmer

Brian, my buddy:
This isn't the end. So I won't
make it sound like one. It's
been a helluva year: remember,
next year, well, not next year,
but still the summer of '02 I'll be
your neihbor, well, not next door
neighbor, but I'll be in the next
town over, across the tracks and up
the hill (riht behind the landfill)
you'll have to come over and party!
I'll always be your friend.
                              Gloria

Brian:
Well, here we are. Even though you never said
anything to me ever, ~~xxxxxxxxxxxx~~ and made
fun of me and my uncle's cleft pallette,
I still think its been great getting to know
you. Stay sweet and good looking and
you've got it made.
                  -- E.L.B.

I SIGNED YOUR CRACK! HaHa

1999 Peepsville High School

Home of the Vengeful Guinea Pigs

"We Got Class!"

Students

Chillin' with my Peeps!

CeeCee Ampere

Aidan Appetizer

Lettie Astor

Brigitte Barndoor

Bubba Barton

Biff Beale

Soiji Benson

Leonid Bisquicke
Worth Blandkins

Everybody learns at their own pace.

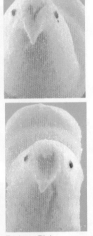
Barbara Blob
Bernice Blob

Blinky Blob

Eaton Boint

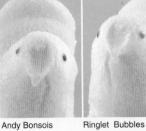
Andy Bonsois

Ringlet Bubbles

No photo available

Ophelia Bumstead

Ginger Breadman

Bitzi Brownie

Billy Bunny

Bibs Carnauba

Roseanne Carnauba

Sonnyann Cher

Sue Chips

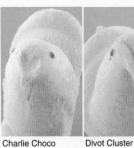

Charlie Choco

Divot Cluster

Iris Colander

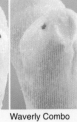

Waverly Combo

Tony Contralto

Grace Crapper

Carlos Crumbles

Chase D'Candy

Willem DeCandy

Daniel Dextrose

G.I. Didit

Arlene Dollops

Oliva Dollops

Hezekiah Downer

Samantha Drizzle

Durwood Drizzle

Endora Drizzle

Justin Earsnoog

Edith Easter

Elizabeth Easter

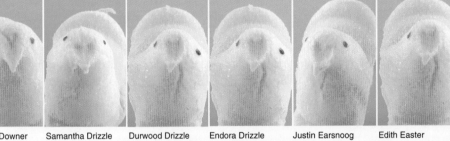

Enid Easter

Erin Easter

Eva Easter

Steve Eatic

Goode Eaton

Blankie Egg

Pilon Esquiviche

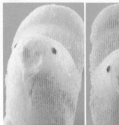

Connie Fection

Jeanette Festoon

Frances Fewcalories

Art Flavors

Rita Flentpoink

Norman Floater

Alice Fluff

 Sally Forth

 Magellan Foster III

 DeDe Fragonnard

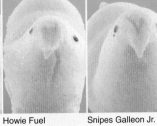 Howie Fuel

 Snipes Galleon Jr.

 Jody Gelatin

Judy Gelatin

 Henry Gooey-Mez

Lisa Gorgonzola

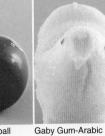 Bryant Gumball

Gaby Gum-Arabic

Grace Gum-Arabic

Roman Halliday

Susan Honeydrop

 Bob Hop

 Aleana Inquisition

 Mary Jo Jollyjelly

Agnostic Jones

 H.P. Jones

Scoobs Juajaki

 Julius Juicyfruits

Edgar Kalorie

Jose Kawasaki

Hillary Kornsyrup

Killian Kornsyrup

Mary Krasbiff

Kimberly Krumbles

Upton Lagasso

 Brandon Q. Larch

 Edith Largesse

 Les Lewis

 Devin D. Licious

 Tor Limbonubbins

 Leslie Limeflavors

 Arte Limfrack

 Elaine Liposucrose

 Jon Lipzowacks

 Renaldo Loaf

Brock Lobster

Luca Lumpagoo

 Dwight Loomink

 Makai Magoo

 Party Martyman

 Kumquat May

 Nibs McCracken

Jim McGoo

Mugs McGoo

Toby McGoo

 Buttress L. McLeod

 Auggie McLumpkin

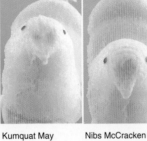 Jésus Melachnik

 Pat E. Melt

Ahmer Meringue

Carie Milkchocowitz

Morkin Minty

 Bill Molasses

 Mallory Moon Pi

 Mark Mashmallow

 Matt Marshmallow

  Golden Moment

Bubb A. Muldoon

   Candy Necklace

Lenore Nostril

 Terri Nothing

 Nester Nougat

 Pat O'Hanlonahan

 Leonid O'Toole

  Ira Oolong

Beth Ort

 Donnie Oozeman

Nicholas Partyman | Brian Peeps | Hobart Peeps | Peggy Peeps | Sugar Peeps | Kiki Pinehurst | Narly Plimpton

Starr Plottsky | Scruggs Plugugly | Maggie Pye | Mattie Pye | Antoine Rabelais | Randolph Randolph | Bailey Ripperton

 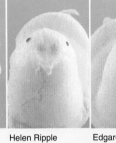  

Hank Ripple | Helen Ripple | Edgardo Roidapol | Darjeeling T. Roint | Siobahn Rolodex | Peter N. Rumball | Latoya Seaton

Henry Scoliosis | Tina Scungilli | Ryan Simpleshape | Ronette Slather | Martin L. Snippet | Linkton O. Snobb | Lothar Soiltoon

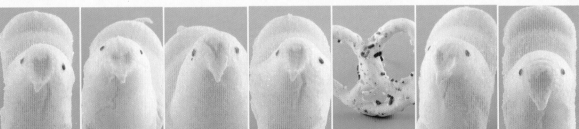  

Gretchen Soda | Silas Softbelly | Polly Sorbate | Waldorf Sorbet | Katie Sparkles | Sofia Sparkles | Michael Sprinkles

School Spirit

Official school mascot Dominic—don't get on his bad side!

"Go Guinea Pigs, go!
Our challenger loses and weeps!
Go Guinea Pigs, go!
We are the victorious Peeps!"

 Betty Sucrose

 Jessica Sugarbeak

Patrick Sugarbeak

Shea Sugarbottom

Simon Sugarman

Ernest T. Swass

 Isabelle Sweetling

 Xavier Swazibutte

 Junior Swizzle

Shirley Syrup

 Brenda Terrebone

Jeff Toad

Teddy Toothsome

 Trent Treat

Tricker Treat

Nestor Trickle

Juanita Tschlingen

Honey Tupper

Fred Turbo

Ima Tush

Plankton Twaddle

 Prissy Twister

 Shirley Uberroth

 Vinny Vanilla

Marianne Void

Ralph Waldo

 Fletcher Watanabe

Anne Wemsmeer

Foamy Wigg

 Shirley Wood

B.D. Yserman

  Thomas Yummystuff

 Hymie Zucker

 Clyde Zamboni Jr.

 Keifer Xorbitol

Homecoming

The Royal Court (left to right): King Buttress L. McLeod, Queen Sugar Peeps, Princess Sofia Sparkles.

Ms. Klumpp supervises decoration details.

Watch your step, Melanie!

Faculty

Brick Halvah, Principal

Leonard Pontoone, Math

Band

Marching to the beat of a different drummer.

Jazz combo: Ain't nobody here but us chicks.

Drama

Drama Club members Hank Ripple and Mary Krasbiff put finishing touches on the set of *Sweet Jambalaya Memories*.

No photo available

Junior Swizzle directs a cast of 1,213 in last year's Peepsville High production of *Nicholas Nickelby*.

Jealous rivalry makes for good humor in *Rivalité, jalousie, humour*. Puérilité!

Peepsville High's new class ring.

Cafeteria Staff

Salad days with the staff (left to right): Yolanda Nut, Jeff Niblet, and Carol Syrup.

Secretaries

"No, I don't give out escalator passes!"
—Janice Kowalski

E. Nadine J. Nightengale

Varsity Sports

Track

Cricket captain "Sam Dunk" Peeps

Diving

¡Fútbol!

Swimming

Showing our school spirit

Clubs

Clubbing

Chess Club

Internet Surf Club

EXTRA!

Peeps Family Trapped in Chocolate Egg Hideaway

Notorious Rodent Apprehended, Leads Detectives to Kidnapped Candie

RAPA NUI — Local authorities are unable to free the prominent Peeps family, trapped since Tuesday inside a chocolate egg. "George Peeps knows how to build them strong," said Detective Ryan Zachary, whose expert sleuthing led to the family's discovery. "I never thought a chocolate hideaway could be so impenetrable."

Last night, Dominic the guinea pig was apprehended as he enjoyed mountain grasses on the slopes of Rano Kau, one of Easter Island's largest volcanoes. "Dominic is very clever," said Zachary. "He was well camouflaged and would have re-

mained hidden if he had better control of his bodily functions. Let's just say he left a trail."

While Dominic was being processed for deportation to Peepsville, Zachary noticed chocolate smears on the rodent's hairy forearms. "It was just a hunch, but I remembered that George Peeps has been constructing a posh chocolate hideaway on the slopes of Rano Kau. We drove out to the work site for a second look. There were several huge chocolate eggs in various states of completion. My suspicions were aroused by one egg which had been sealed before any doors or

windows were installed. I put my ear to the chocolate and heard faint bickering noises from within. It could only be the missing Peeps family. Everyone knows George and Crystal love to bicker."

Zachary deduces that Dominic must have pushed the chocolate egg closed while the family was inspecting the richly detailed interior. "Everyone knows that guinea pigs hold grudges. Dominic must have hidden behind a nearby moai and waited until the family was perfectly positioned. Then he pushed the other half of the egg into place with his strong

EXTRA!

Dominic: Recidivist rodent.

Sugar-coated sleuth: Detective Ryan Zachary locates the imperiled Peeps.

forearms. The hot Rapa Nui sunshine would have melded the egg together in a flash."

Rescue crews have been working nonstop to free the trapped family, but so far the chocolate egg remains hopelessly sealed. "We simply don't have the strength or technology to break apart the chocolate," confessed Detective Zachary. "We're calling on our best minds to help free the Peeps. It won't be long before they granulate."

4:00 p.m.: Now that both children are in school, Mother is plotting her return to Wall Street.

EXTRA!

Peepsville Residents Rally Around Imperiled Peeps

Bake sales, Benefits Scheduled to Raise Funds for High-Tech Laser

PEEPSVILLE — Local residents are uniting to raise funds to build Dr. Rosebud Roberts's Chocolaser 3000, the experimental chocolate-breaking device she has developed in conjunction with her star pupil, Cocoa the Cat. Residents hope that the weapon can be constructed, candy coated, and shipped to Easter Island in time to save the Peeps family from their airless chocolate-egg prison.

"I'm so glad that the good folks of Peepsville have placed their trust in our genius invention," said Dr. Roberts from her lab at the Marshmallow Treat Foundation. "When I told

Cocoa about the trapped family, she used American Candy Language to sign 'Baby sugar knuckle yum yum.' Loosely translated, that means 'Let's build that Chocolaser 3000 you've been talking about, Dr. Roberts. We must use our superior intelligence to free the Peeps family.'"

A prototype of the laser has failed to function properly, but Dr. Roberts believes a solution is close at hand. "I'm a firm believer in throwing money at a problem. I don't need to mention that I'm one of the few people around here with a throwing arm, do I? Anyway, this is a big problem, so we're

going to need lots of cash. I'm guessing seventy-three million dollars and sixty-two cents should suffice, as long as it's in nonsequential, unmarked bills and coins. We're only charging for parts, so when you think about it, seventy-three million dollars and change isn't much to pay."

Tomorrow night, folk legend Runyon Peep Jones will headline a benefit concert at the Peepsville Arena.

Residents of the Crystal Dish Retirement Facility are planning a rummage sale of dusty knickknacks. Crystal Dish manager Ginger Breadman promises that *Peep Idol*

EXTRA!

Rosie O'Doughnut: "I'm wholly committed to saving the Peeps family!"

loser Darla Fondant will not be on hand to perform karaoke favorites. "We don't want to scare away business," said Breadman. "It's for a very good cause, plus I need folks to cart away this useless junk. My dust allergies are horrendous."

Funny pastry Rosie O'Doughnut is preparing a large dish of her famous sweet-potato smoothies. "It's for the charity bake sale," said O'Doughnut. "We've got to save those little cuties!"

Museum of Peeps Art officials have announced plans to auction off one of their most beloved paintings. "Folks love *Peep with a Pearl Earring*," says Museum Director Philpeep de Marshmallow. "But George Peeps designed this gorgeous museum, so the least we can do is sell off our number-one attraction in order to support the questionable schemes of Dr. Rosebud Roberts. Besides, we'll probably find a valuable replacement painting at the Crystal Dish Retirement Facility's rummage sale."

I really need a break from my housework . . .
COCOA'S CANDY LANGUAGE:
"yum yum knuckle sugar baby yum!"
PLUS:

BRAD PEEP
Learns to say "yes," "no," and "harumph!"

JENNIFER CORDUROY
Diagnosis: Fun!

SHARK ATTA
Who knew sh
liked marshn

s:
K
OFFICE
be & Kevin
cKor on the
oys of raising
the quints

contents

16 FEATURE

Bebe and Kevin
McKor on the joys
and sorrows of raising
Cleveland, Niles,
Warren, Akron
Canton, and
Little Columbus.

ON THE COVER: Sugar Peeps makes a splash in
her garden. Photograph by Mortimer. Gown by
Olivia. Makeup by Shalimark.

MailBag

McKOR QUINTUPLETS

Am I the only peep who's tired of hearing about the lousy McKor Quintuplets? So they were extruded together as a joined set of five. Big deal. Where's the miracle? Don't they all come out that way? My sister Dawn has offset eyes but she manages quite well. I've enclosed a photograph. Why don't you write a story about her? I'd pay to read it, that's for sure.
Billy Bunny, *Peepsville*

I'm a huge fan of celebrities and all they do for important charities, so my heart practically melted when I read that Brad Peep had purchased a gorgeous ranch-style home for the McKor Quintuplets. Those youngsters certainly deserve loads of publicity, praise, and free gifts. They are a true candy-making miracle!
Sharon Shatner, *Chicago, IL*

DOMINIC THE GUINEA PIG

Now that Dominic's outrageous imprisonment has come to an end, I'm glad he'll be able to get back to some semblance of a normal life at home with his master, Mandrake Peeps. It's terribly unfair that he must be shackled with those embarrassing ankle bracelets. Everyone knows Dominic is completely innocent. Why would the gentle giant eat a marshmallow Christmas treat? Perhaps no one will ever know what really happened to the Municipal Christmas Tree, but I'll never believe Dominic devoured

the seasonal favorite. Crystal Peeps should admit her fib. She loves to stir up trouble!
Nelson Clusters, *Burlington, VT.*

I can't believe they're letting Dominic serve out his prison sentence at home! A jury of his Peeps concluded that he'd developed a taste for marshmallow. He has giant sharp teeth. Isn't anyone worried that he might gnaw through his ankle bracelets? If I were Crystal Peeps, I would sleep with one eye open! Guinea pigs are nothing if not vengeful.
Katherine Reed, *Niles, OH*

Enough with Dominic the guinea pig! I thought this magazine was about Peeps? Last I heard, they don't make guinea-pig-shaped Peeps! Thank goodness for small favors!
Carol Gerkin Forbes, *Coral Gables, FL*

OLD FASHIONED PEEPS

Thanks for your beautiful story on forgotten Peeps of the 1940s. They don't make them like they used to, that's for sure! I particularly enjoyed the update on the Rodda Sisters. Darlene, Marlene, and Peeplene still look plenty gorgeous to these jaded eyes! Their sweet vocal harmonies kept us chirping through challenging times. They might have been squeezed through a pastry tube, but I'd still choose their handcrafted charm over these assembly-line starlets of today!
Lorenzo Menzies, *Oswego, IL*

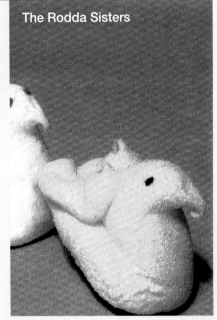

The Rodda Sisters

[Editor's note: The Rodda Sisters are residents at Peepsville's Crystal Dish Retirement Facility. They welcome your cards and letters!]

What's with these modern Peeps who run around town in outlandish colors like blue and lavender? Call me old-fashioned, but what's wrong with pink, yellow, and white? Back in the olden days, proper Peeps didn't put on such airs. No, they were content to spend quiet afternoons in their lovely baskets, exchanging pleasantries with the chocolate rabbits and jelly beans. As a cellophane-wrapped hard candy, I admired the way they kept themselves out of sticky situations. These newfangled Peeps are asking for trouble with their dazzling hues!
Hazel Dugan, *Peepsville*

In your November 13 issue you spelled the word "obstreperous" incorrectly. It should have read "obstreperous."
Lonnie R. Dingle III, *Ralston, VA*

Scoop

POP QUIZ

Sugar Peeps

In *Peep with a Pearl Earring*, Sugar plays Meep, an innocent maid who works in the household of a talented seventeenth-century painter. After appearing in a series of critical and commercial flops, Sugar's dazzling performance in *Pearl Earring* is being heralded as nothing short of an amazing comeback. Sugar, 25, has been nominated for a Peeple's Choice Award. She spoke by telephone from Easter Island, where she is filming the highly anticipated *Jurassic Peep* with Brad Peep and Peeper Sutherland.

How does it feel to be the top chick at the box office once more?
It feels great, silly. Try not to waste my valuable time with such foolish questions.

Your acting choices are very eclectic.
Well, Meryl Peep is my idol, and she proves that a Peep can tackle a wide variety of roles.

Your family must be very proud of you.
Actually, my mother didn't want me to portray Meep. [Sugar's mother is Crystal Peeps, host of PEEPS Television's *Sweet Nothings.*] She thought I couldn't afford the risk. "You're America's sweetheart," she said. "Peeps don't want to see you in frumpy dramatic roles. You need to sparkle."

You're best known for fluff roles in sugary romantic comedies.
Maybe so, but I'm more than just a sugary confection. Of course, I taste good in Easter baskets, but I want to be respected for my good taste in acting roles, too. In *Jurassic Peep*, I escape a T. rex by hiding inside Peeper Sutherland's mouth. He wanted to shoot the scene over and over!

You must be excited to be shooting Jurassic Peep on Easter Island.
I love it here! I feel right at home among the mysterious *moai* and volcanic rocks.

What makes you happy?
Puppies, bunnies, the smell of a Just Born baby's skin fresh from the extrusion module, world peace, big piles of warm laundry, the look in the eyes of the downtrodden when I lovingly administer malaria medicine—served up with a dollop of caramel, of course.

How do you handle the stress of being a big movie star?
I don't wilt under pressure. In fact, my sugary coating doesn't begin to melt until I reach 212 degrees Fahrenheit. Besides, I'm kind of like a duck. It all rolls off my back.

You've achieved a certain renown in the celebrity press . . .
Am I a bit demanding? Well, I'm just looking out for Sugar. Is a refrigerator stocked with Gallo Brut Sparkling Cider and chocolate covered lingonberries too much to ask?

. . . And I've heard pillows?
A star must be comfortable. And not another word about the lingonberries, okay? I don't want to make my other friends jealous. There's only so much room in that fridge.

ON THE BLOCK

GEORGE PEEPS'S SHOW PACKET
PRICE: About $2.4 million
PLACE: Warren, OH
George Peeps designed this classic flat for Runyon Peep Jones in 1962.

jodie frosting / frosty brooks / brick sweets / anthony hoppinjohn

the silence of the peeps

from the sweetly terrifying best-seller

a malodorous picture / jodie frosting / frosty brooks / brick sweets / anthony hoppinjohn / "the silence of the peeps" / jeff naugahyde / music by tørge ripstop / production designer hooligan c. dullard
director of perspicacity jed nuggwagon / edited by uncle tina jr., A.C.E. / executive producer simon simpleton / based on a lump of marshmallow by duffer sagbottom / screenplay by oscillate m. snodgrass /
produced by hoagy melanoma III AND nubs mcface / directed by elinore haggis, ltd.

Those Amazing McKor Quintuplets!

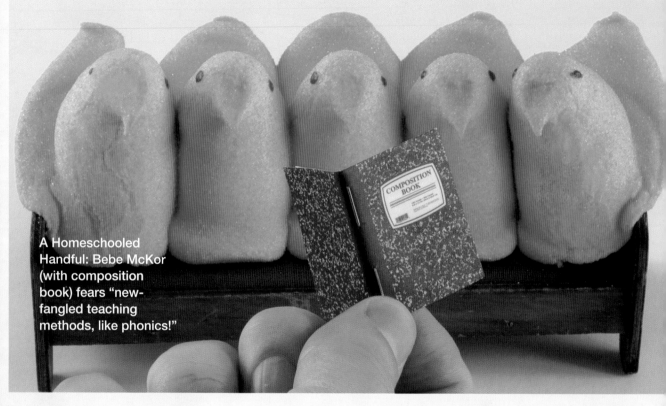

A Homeschooled Handful: Bebe McKor (with composition book) fears "new-fangled teaching methods, like phonics!"

It's been five years since the McKor Quintuplets were extruded, but folks are still fascinated by these amazing confections! Cleveland, Niles, Warren, Akron Canton, and Little Columbus McKor might be universally beloved, but no one cherishes them more than their proud adoptive parents.

Bebe and Kevin McKor of Bethlehem, Pennsylvania, had tried in vain to produce a batch but were thwarted by a lack of expertise, equipment, and common sense.

"They look so easy to make," says Bebe, a 28-year-old semiprofessional lawn globe polisher. "But man, we were getting so frustrated! Kevin's grandmother gave us a secondhand fondue pot for our wedding. It was well rusted and had some hardened cheese and sausage stuck to the bottom. Just like Kevin! Ha ha ha. In other words, it was seasoned to perfection. We thought we could cook up our favorite marshmallow candies."

Kevin, 29, a semiemployed candy striper at Peepsville's Crystal Dish Retirement Facility, shudders at the memory. "Many folks swear by their fondue pots, but I'm afraid I swore *at* mine. Those contraptions are dangerous!"

Bebe and Kevin donned protective earmuffs and attempted to melt a bag of miniature marshmallows in the sputtering appliance. "I read the ingredients for Peeps and it said there was carnauba wax in there," remembers Bebe. "Well, we didn't have any of that, and I'd used up my last scented beeswax candle at the Kenny G concert. The only kind of wax I could find was inside Kevin's ear holes, so I drilled a few tunnels through his earmuffs until I found the openings. I buried my finger in there about three, four inches. After a little digging, I pulled out a big yellow plum. It melted okay but the smell wasn't as tempting as you'd like."

Kevin thought he could mold the melted mixture by hand. First he tried dipping his fingers into the steaming concoction. "It was very painful," he murmurs. "I destroyed our aloe plant, rubbing its soothing emollients into my burnt flesh." Finally, he donned an oven glove and managed to pull out a mittful of the unsavory beige goo.

"It didn't look like anything because we didn't have a pastry bag," says Kevin. "Then Bebe had a great idea. She cut a tiny hole at the bottom of her support hose and we put the marshmallow mess in there. I tried squeezing it out, but it oozed through the mesh, plus it was burning Bebe's leg. Dang, we were flustered! Our Easter Sunday was ruined. To comfort ourselves, we ate a large dish of loose sugar and went to bed."

Three weeks later, Kevin's grandmother gave the couple a specially discounted Easter basket packed to the brim with aged goodies, including a cellophane-wrapped package of Peeps chicks. "It was miraculous," says Bebe. "There were five little chicks all stuck together. They were so beautiful. After our difficulties with the fondue pot and the support hose, we'd given up hope. What a blessing!"

Bebe's eyes swell with tears of joy. "Of course, we alerted the press. They couldn't believe how excited we were. They said we were incredible imbeciles! Well, kind words go a long way with us, but we held out for complimentary scratch 'n' match lottery tickets before we agreed to appear on the evening news! Our neighbors were thrilled with our good fortune and volunteered to help us raise the little darlings. It takes a village, after all."

While many people would feel confused by the task of nurturing Marshmallow Peeps, the McKors rose to the challenge. "Any one can polish lawn globes and paint stripes on candy," says Kevin. "It takes a special sort to care for Marshmallow Peeps."

Now that the quints are five, life in the McKor home is settling into a more relaxed routine. "At first we hardly slept," admits Bebe. "We had to watch those chicks like hawks. You know how our neighbors said they wanted to help us? Well, it turns out they had more sinister plans!"

Kevin shakes his head in disgust. "Those monsters! Luckily, actor Brad Peep heard about our plight and bought us a gorgeous ranch-style home in Peepsville. Bebe was thrilled. The public schools are terrific so she isn't forced to homeschool any longer. It's wonderful to live in a community where everyone shares our wholesome values."

By Jimbo Snuggles in Peepsville

Bebe and Kevin spend quality time with their quintuplets.

StyleWatch

Good Taste and Tastes Good, Too!

Check out these candy store confections! Yum yum!

First-class dress dummy Xenia Peeps dazzles in a slinky licorice string ensemble!

Meryl Peep is oodles and oodles of frothy fun!

Sugar Peeps, making waves on Rapa Nui!

Blankie Egg is poached perfection in Humpty's hand-me-downs!

StyleWatch

Spit it Out! Yuck!

We pity these poorly dressed Peeps!

What was she thinking??

Darla Fondant is a mesclun mess!

Katie Bunny is a catastrophe in condiment couture!

Crystal Peeps is *too too old* for a tutu!

Ada Peeps is *for the birds* in this long-necked nightmare!

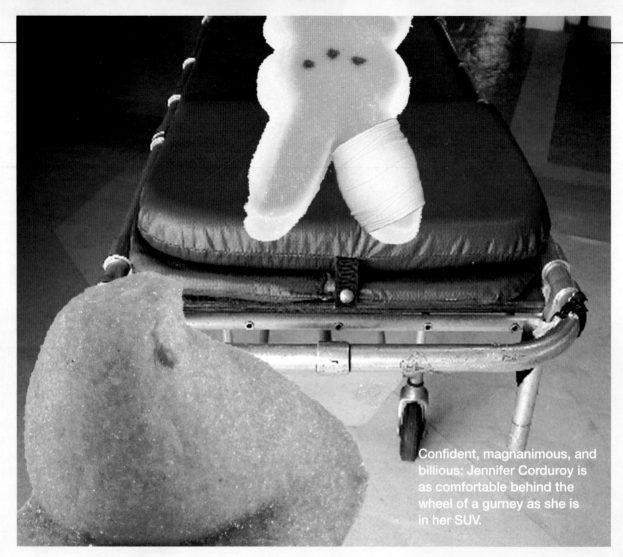

Confident, magnanimous, and billious: Jennifer Corduroy is as comfortable behind the wheel of a gurney as she is in her SUV.

Jennifer Corduroy—No Limits!

The young, purple medical student was nervous as she slid the soft, thin tube down into the patient's windpipe. It was a delicate operation, and she knew the patient's life depended on her nerves of sucrose.

Jennifer Corduroy III leaned over the patient as her professor and a team of others closely monitored her every move. Care-fully, she positioned the tube, beady brown eyes looking for the special signal that oxygen was flowing.

The anesthesia machine was set to emit pear-shaped tones to confirm that the tube was in the trachea and carbon dioxide was present. Soon, Corduroy heard the sounds. She double-checked with a stethoscope. All was okay. She had successfully completed the intubation.

Several times over two weeks, Corduroy performed this difficult task at the North-Western East New Jersey Hospital and Clinics. Her professor, Dr. Clyde Marmot, marveled at his student's skills.

"She was 109 percent," the doc-tor says. "She did it better than the interns who were human."

Profile

Jennifer Corduroy III is a Peep.

She has mastered much in her 28 years: Jujitsu. Biotaxonometry. Surfing. Jello wrestling. Any one of these accomplishments would be impressive. Together, they're bedazzling. And now, there's more luster for her sequined resume with a new title: Doctor.

Corduroy has earned her MD.

In a world where skeptics always seem to be saying, "Stop, this isn't something a sponge treat should be doing," it was one more barrier overcome. There are only a handful of candy doctors in this country. But Corduroy makes it clear she could not have joined this elite club alone.

"I signed on with a bunch of balls-out dessert cakes who decided that things are only impossible until they're done," she says.

That's modesty speaking. Corduroy finished medical school at the North-Western East New Jersey Hospital and Clinics in the top seventeenth of her class (she received just one D–), earning honors, accolades, and admirers along the way.

"She was confident, she was magnanimous, she was billious, and she was a great bowler," says Belinda Flagellan, a nurse practitioner who worked with Corduroy as part of a training program in a small-town clinic.

At a paltry 3.25 inches tall, and without hands, Corduroy had to learn how to identify clusters of rhubarb-thin veins and celery-green nerves in cadavers, study X rays, read EEGs and patient charts, examine multiple-choice slides showing slices of the brain and pizza, diagnose rashes—and more. "The biggest ordeal, believe it or not, is overcoming the effects of formaldehyde on my sugary coating. It's awful, and stinks," she lamented.

She used a variety of special tools, including potato peelers, Lincoln Logs, a computer that simulates mambo dance steps, and a device called a hydro-syruptometer.

"It was kind of whatever worked," Corduroy says. "Sometimes you can psych yourself out and anticipate problems that don't materialize. You can grab what's handy, like the time I needed to resuscitate this dude and had a polo mallet and some cream cheese in my bag. I love to improvise."

That's been her philosophy much of her life. Corduroy was just 5 months old when she was diagnosed with degenerative fructasis, a condition that caused her skin to resemble the charred surface of crème brûlée. She constantly had to administer various jam and jelly ointments and was force-fed a diet of sucrose pellets in the shape of big land mines. At age 16, when her peers were getting their car keys, she found chunks of her scalp falling off in her oatmeal.

Still, marshmallow-pattern baldness didn't stop her.

She wrestled and earned a magenta belt in tae kwon do and jujitsu. An academic whiz, she won the tag-team crown at competitive Yahtzee as a crowd of 10,000 gave her a standing ovation.

Corduroy finished medical school in December but still is working on her PhD, studying the structure of a protein involved in a bacteria that causes pneumonia and other infections.

By E. Jiggers Dirt in Peepsville

In his new memoir, ageless pop star Runyon Peep Jones reveals the honeyed voice beneath the glossy rock (candy) star exterior . . . or does he?

Runyon Peep Jones: A Memoir

I woke up one morning in the muggy heat of an over-stuffed living room. I found myself in an unfamiliar candy bowl, surrounded by strange fruit. Actually, it was a fruit bowl and somewhere in the wild night of my twenty-second birthday I went terribly astray. Ashtrays were piled with butts, butts were smoking and there was . . . My sugary coating had been removed and I was there in all my spongy vulnerability. My little brown eyes were opened wide as they could be, and there was no turning back.

It was an awakening like no other, and my senses were atingle. Two apples flanked me, shiny and blush in the morning light. Some-where a polka played.

I untangled myself from between three red Hot Tamales and a long dark licorice limb that had put that numbness into my torso and made my way to the bathroom. My guitar was on the floor under a pair of briefs and the neck and strings were sticky with marmalade. Just then the chord structure of what was to become "A Hard Shell's Gonna Crumble" slid back into my mind like a chocolatey slide guitar glissando. I madly jotted lyrics on an old towel as I reapplied sugar to my cheeks in the mirror. I must have been humming too loud because I heard the sounds of Cocoa and others stirring in the kitchen.

Just as I was about to lather up with whipped cream for another round of shaving I began thinking about some of my heroes: Wigwam Jones, Shirley Jones, Grandpa Jones, whom I consider the greatest songwriter of all time. The story of his countless hours of woodshedding with his 75-cent guitar, a 5-cent cigar, and strange looks at the girls from afar, man, that was what I wanted to be. I ran out and bought myself a pair of suspenders and wire-rimmed eyeglasses and memorized his catalog. When I heard he was sick in the hospital, I made a pilgrimage to his bedside. I'll never forget the cross-eyed, morphined-up look on his face when I ripped into a rendition of "An Answer to the Maple on the Hill," and when I finished with "It's Raining Here This Morning" I saw a tear form in his eye. He asked me for another hit of morphine and whispered in my ear, "You're a sweet kid." Walking home after that summit meeting through the rain and muck I got splashed by a bus alongside the highway and my suspenders shrunk so far my marshmallow shoulder compressed all the way to my ass. But I'll never ever live up to his standard of excellence in songwriting.

I decided to try a harmonica, but not just any harmonica. You know those friendly harmonicas, the ones everybody loves? Who can resist a friendly harmonica? It makes you feel all warm and syrupy. Well, that ain't the kind of harmonica I wanted. I wanted the kind that makes the sugar grains just want to fall right off you. That was it. When I play live, I want folks to feel like they're leaving a little piece of themselves right on the floor when they leave. As a performer I do that. So that harmonica screams, man. It's not sweet, but it sure gets my [sic] 'cane goin' and my fructose flowin.' Not everybody liked that, though.

RUNYON
PEEP
JONES
LACTOSE
INTOLERANCE
BLUES

I Shall Be Extruded

They say ev'rything can be
  included,
Yet ev'ry distance is not near.
So I remember ev'ry face
Ev'ry trick-or-treater who put me
  here.
I see my light come shining
From inside of the big metal
  machine.
Any day now, any day now,
I shall be extruded.

They say ev'ry man is deluded,
They say ev'ry man must fall.
Yet I swear I see my reflection
Someplace so high above this
  mixer.
I see my light come shining
  'til my sweet 'mallow is denuded,
Any day now, any day now,
I shall be extruded.

Standing next to me in this lonely
  bowl,
Is a man who swears he's not too
  sweet.
All day long I hear him shout so
  loud,
Saccharine eyes cry so sweetly,
I see my light come shining
  'til my laptop is rebooted,
Any day now, any day now,
I shall be extruded.

Interview

CRYSTAL PEEPS: CANDY ICON

Crystal Peeps before cosmetic enhancement. "I'm well past my sell-by date!"

Crystal Peeps has recently published her autobiography, Peeps Will Talk, *a fluff piece about her years as Peepsville's most beloved talk show hostess. While the tabloid press has made much of Crystal's inflammatory accusations and shocking revelations,* Peeple *Editor-in-Chief* **Buster Buttons** *was surprised to encounter a relaxed, gracious confection. "While she might be the most successful non-chocolate Easter candy of her generation, Crystal is certainly a polarizing figure," says Buttons. "Some folks are revolted by her sugary manner, while others can't get enough of her glistening goodness. I was surprised by her emotional vulnerability and her willingness to share her deepest thoughts and emotions."*

BUSTER: You look amazing, Crystal. How do you maintain such a youthful appearance?

CRYSTAL: I've had extensive work, sweetheart. Time is merciless! Believe me, I'm well past my sell-by date! We fight it, but one day you wake up and your marshmallow filling is hard, maybe you find some extra sugar crystals on the pillowcase. Some folks prefer us a little on the aged side, but they're in the minority. Listen, I'm not ashamed to talk about my cosmetic adventures.

Everything I've done has been for my own happiness. Well, actually, I've been trying to win back my husband's attention. As you well know, he's been spotted around town with Prissy Twister, the chocolate-covered pretzel who picks up his laundry. Anyway, looking good makes me feel good. And that's what counts, right? A nip here, a tuck there, a few milliliters of corn syrup injected about the eyes, and I'm sweet as the day I was extruded.

BUSTER: You've had your ups and downs.

CRYSTAL: That's true. But what anthropomorphized candy icon hasn't? Look at Mike and Ike. Their faces might be forgotten, but they're more popular

Crystal Peeps (at home) isn't ashamed to discuss her cosmetic enhancements. "I look tasty!" she brags.

than ever. Those guys are real troopers.

BUSTER: How has your family helped you through the rough patches?

CRYSTAL: I love them dearly, but they've brought me my share of heartache. Sugar is still angry because I put her up for adoption last year. She said, "You can't do that, I'm fully grown." But I said, "Sugar, if you continue to make terrible films like *The Breakfast Peep* and *Peep, Interrupted*, what alternative do you leave me? A candy icon can't afford to associate with box office poison." Luckily, she took my advice and accepted the role of Meep in *Peep with a Pearl Earring*. Anyway, those bad feelings are all behind us now. Actually, I'm going to join her on Easter Island next week. She's wrapping up work on *Jurassic Peep* and we're going to relax and enjoy spa treatments together. The whole family is reuniting. It's going to be beautiful. Of course, I'll film the entire trip so I can share it with my many fans. Be sure to tune in to *Sweet Nothings* next week for live coverage!

BUSTER: Spoken like a true television legend! Incidentally, how did you convince George and Brian to join you?

CRYSTAL: Well, George is already on the island, supervising the construction of a posh resort. It will be the world's first solid chocolate hideaway. And Brian works as Sugar's nutritionist. He supervises her diet.

BUSTER: Has widespread ridicule damaged your son? As a candy nutritionist, he's a laughingstock.

CRYSTAL: I'm so proud of Brian. Isn't that what I'm supposed to say? Anyway, he keeps a low profile. He doesn't go around blabbing about our "vitamin deficiencies" anymore. He's matured. Whatever we lack in vitamins, we more than make up for in fun!

BUSTER: Why did you refuse to fund his college education?

CRYSTAL: We're pragmatists. We felt Brian should study something with practical applications, like sugar spinning or taffy pulling. Who ever heard of a candy nutritionist?

BUSTER: Brian paid his way through school by participating in countless disfiguring scientific experiments. Did you feel guilty watching him submit to such hardships?

CRYSTAL: Heavens, no! Brian has thanked us countless times for the many hurdles and roadblocks we set up in his way. He always bounces back. Brian has the con-

A few days at the spa helps Crystal unwind and get back that glistening, sugary glow.

fidence that comes from knowing he's made of the right stuff— sugar, corn syrup, and gelatin! After all, isn't it wonderful to have the inner resources to make one's own way in this cruel world?

BUSTER: Why are you bickering with your husband? Clearly, you're made for each other.

CRYSTAL: Well, life is sweet and sour, isn't it? George has been

with Miss Twister. He claims to be distracted by his work on the Easter Island Resort. Apparently, he's devised some novel chocolate construction techniques.

CRYSTAL: I hope that's true, Buster. Anyway, I'm not taking any chances. I'm not going to let some twisted salty-sweet vixen steal my man! I visited Dr. Jennifer Corduroy at the Peepsville Clinic

I made up the whole story. People who believe I paid some unscrupulous characters to cart the Christmas tree away. But I know what I saw, and I didn't see Mike and Ike loading the tree in the back of their vaudevillian surrey. No, I saw a monstrous rodent devouring the municipal Christmas tree! I wasn't about to let Dominic get away with ruining our Christ-

spending too much time at the office. Last week, I noticed a smear of chocolate on his collar. I was crushed. I immediately surmised that he had fallen against the crossed arms of Prissy Twister, the chocolate-covered pretzel who sometimes works as our travel agent. Admittedly, her curves are quite fetching.

BUSTER: I think we need to point out that George vehemently denies any romantic entanglements

and she improvised beauty treatments. I feel great!

BUSTER: What are your hopes for the trip to Easter Island? You're aware that many candies believe it's a cynical grab for ratings.

CRYSTAL: Let candies believe what they wish! You don't become an icon by giving up on love and family. Folks have doubted my intentions in the past. Remember the trial of Dominic the guinea pig? There are still people who believe

mas spirit. Can I help it if grateful viewers rewarded my talk show with monster ratings?

BUSTER: Maybe not, but watch your back! Many folks believe Dominic is plotting his revenge.

CRYSTAL: That's silly. He's a guinea pig.

BUSTER: Have a great time on Easter Island. We'll be watching!

With Cosgrove Groin III in Peepsville

Spotlight on Brian Peeps

I t's fun to mock Brian Peeps. He's a nutritionist, for Peeps' sake! Still, this marshmallow's got moxie. With no financial support from his wealthy parents, Brian paid for college by participating in research experiments. Here's an exclusive look at Brian's shocking medical files!

Dandruff shampoo test

Microwave endurance test 62 seconds

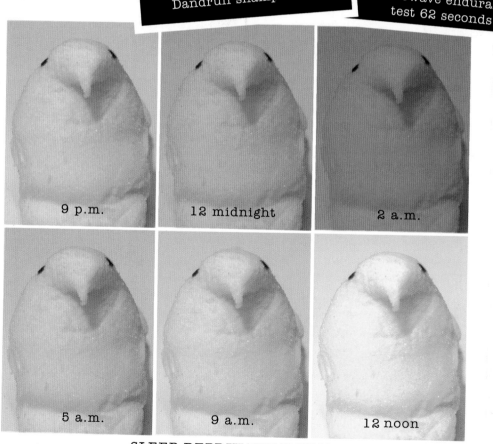

9 p.m.

12 midnight

2 a.m.

5 a.m.

9 a.m.

12 noon

SLEEP DEPRIVATION TEST

PEEPSVILLE UNIVERSITY
DEPARTMENT OF CANDY SCIENCE

Subject Name: _Brian Peeps_

Age: _19_

Height: _3.875 inches_

Calories: _32_

Emergency Contact: _Crystal Peeps (mother) (123) 555-PEEP_

Subject Classification (check one)

X Workstudy Volunteer

X Academic Probation (Please note Extra Credit points accrued: _62_)

___ Cadaver

This subject has participated in the following Studies/Experiments:

Dandruff Shampoo Test

Freshness Test

Taste Test

Sleep Deprivation Test

Symmetry Test

IN CASE OF EMERGENCY, DO NOT RESUSCITATE

Crystal Peeps

AUTHORIZED SIGNATURE

AroundTown

Sugar, everyone's favorite candy actress, was spotted at the Yum Yum Club enjoying yogurt-covered raisins with newly single **Brad Peep**. "Sugar looked gorgeous," said one star-struck observer. "Pricey candy necklaces accentuated her glistening outer shell to perfection. She was dancing on the tabletops and striking provocative poses. Well, imagine my shock when Sugar lifted her wings and revealed a thick nest of underarm hair. Can you believe it? With all her fame and money, you'd think some-one would have taken care of that for her." Representatives for Sugar deny the allegation. "Sugar doesn't even have underarms, so how can she have underarm hair? You crazy Peeps will print anything to sell magazines."

Renée Zellpeeper is roly-poly once more! The enchanting ingenue has been tapped to star in *Runaway Pancake* as a syrup-drenched gal on the go! "Packing on the pounds was hard work," confesses the magnifi-cently mounded morsel. "Luckily, nutritionist **Brian Peeps** devised a high-fat, whole-fudge diet to sup-plement my scant 32-calorie frame. Brian was very encouraging. He force-fed me rich cream pies and twice-baked potatoes. I love being chubby!" Renée also loves being in love. Zellpeeper has recently been linked to sexy pork sausage **Corey Ham**, who portrayed her cantilevered love interest in *The Bridge in Joan's Diorama*.

Fresh Coconut

Poor **Little Columbus McKor**! The littlest member of the famed **McKor Quintuplets** was making

his way into the **CinePeeps Theater** for a recent showing of *The Silence of the Peeps* when an overzealous moviehall worker placed him in the snack case. "It was an honest mistake," said ticket-taker **Lisa Johnson**. "How was I supposed to know he paid to see the movie? I'm making $5.15 an hour, for Peeps' sake. Why can't you folks let me work on my word search in peace? Dang."

Wall-sitter **Blankie Egg**'s May-December romance with Peepsville detective **Larry "Pop" Sicle** has ended. "It just wasn't working out," says the famed clothes-horse. "At the end of the day, we come from different worlds. We were sunbathing on the beach, and all of a sudden, he turned into a puddle. Talk about your high-maintenance boyfriends! Plus, his apartment is freezing."

Seems like **Ada Peeps** is translating her *Peep Idol* win into big-time show-biz success! Insiders say the teen queen is filming a television pilot tentatively titled **Candy Lips, Peep Detective**. Ada plays Candy Lips, a precocious teen who manages to get herself into all kinds of sticky situations. **Florence Peeperson** has signed on to play her cranky adoptive mother. "I love the part," says Peeperson. "In almost every episode, I have to restrain myself from taking a bite out of tasty Candy. Ada is delicious." While folks are buzzing over her newly slender appearance, the sugary sensation is denying allegations she used aspartame to lose calories. "I categorically deny these vicious rumors!" said the angry pop chanteuse. "I'm still just 32 calories. Remember **Darla Fondant**, the big loser from *Peep Idol*? She'll say anything to besmirch my wholesome reputation. She's incredibly jealous of my popularity."

Teen Peep sensation **Hilary Puff** was enjoying spa treatments at the **Peepsville Day Spa** when **Sugar** interrupted her solitude. "I was getting one of those hot-fudge treatments? Like, where they drizzle hot fudge onto your forehead? It's incredibly therapeutic. Anyway, Sugar comes bouncing into the room with about twelve bodyguards—these really big pound cakes, really threatening. And she's like, 'Off the table, Puff. Sugar's here, and Sugar needs a sugar dusting.' I was like, wait your turn, chick. And she was like, 'Sorry, did you say something to me?' Then she ordered those pound cakes to toss me off the table. It was horrible. Sugar was great in **Peep with a Pearl Earring**, but do we really need another candy diva? She's still jealous that I beat her out for the part in **Mean Chicks**. I'm certain to win a **Peeple's Choice Award**.

AroundTown

"This is not your father's *Circus of the Sweets*," confides impresario **P. T. Peepum**, who is producing the eagerly awaited extravaganza for PEEPS Television. "For one thing, it's incredibly dangerous." Peepum wants to change negative perceptions about B-list candy celebrities. "These sweet folks are seriously undervalued," claims Peepum. "Particularly since they're willing to be draped in pork sausages and dropped into a pit of vicious white tigers with only cinnamon sticks for protection." Peepum insists his production will fascinate the entire family. "It's going to be great. Circus peanuts will balance themselves on the tips of hungry elephant trunks, and **Peepscilla Presley** has agreed to twirl by her teeth over a steaming pot of chocolate fondue."

The ever popular **McKor Quintuplets** were spotted at the **Peepsville Zoo**, getting a private tour of the Komodo dragon exhibit. **Cleveland McKor** waddled over to **Clarabell**, a seven-foot endangered Indonesian lizard and was promptly devoured. "It served him right," said **Hazel Dugan**, a cellophane-wrapped hard candy who witnessed the spectacle. "My granddaughter **Rigley** can't sleep at night. 'Grandma,' she says, 'how come the lizard ate Cleveland?' I tried to tell her about the After Taste, but she doesn't understand." Despite eyewitness accounts, Clarabell denies any involvement in Cleveland's disappearance. "I only eat rats," she said. "Personally, I'm sick of those McKor Quints getting special treatment. Anyway, I never invited Cleveland into my cage."

Steppin' out!

The hottest fad in **Peepsville** these days? Word searches! *Peep Idol* star **Peepla Abdul** swears by them. "Ever since I started judging talent shows, nothing relaxes me like a good word search. I've been hosting a weekly word-search night with my celebrity friends. Last week, **Peepscilla Presley** found the word 'popsicle.' It was incredible!"

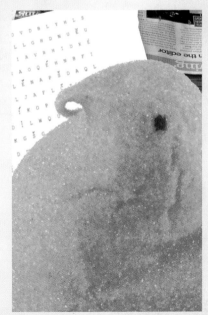

George and Crystal Peeps like to bicker, but you wouldn't know it from their affectionate display at the Yum Yum Club last Thursday. "George and Crystal glittered in matching Western-wear ensembles," says **Meryl Peep**, who was seated at the next table. "George kept picking off bits of Crystal's gorgeous sugar shell and letting them dissolve slowly on his outstretched tongue. They looked as if they were still very much in love."

EXTRA!

The Peeps Are

RAPA NUI — Dominic the guinea pig has rescued the Peeps family from their sealed chocolate hideaway. "He certainly didn't intend to free them," said Detective Ryan Zachary. "Dominic is vengeance incarnate. Fortunately, he's also rather simple."

When Dr. Rosebud Roberts's Chocolaser 3000 failed to materialize, island authorities implemented a dangerous last-ditch rescue. "The capricious cavy was transported to a 'fresh grazing field' for his daily exercise," said Detective Zachary. "We had camouflaged the chocolate hideaway with succulent mountain grasses. Dominic was instantly drawn to the fragrant mound. He ate the vegetation and kept

Dominic: From villified to vindicated?

Life is sweet: The grateful Peeps greet their sharp-toothed savior.

EXTRA!

Free! Heroic Dominic Gnaws Opening in Chocolate Egg

Valiant vegetable: This brave baby carrot distracted Dominic while the Peeps escaped.

Peepsville celebrates: "I'm so happy they're free," said Blankie Egg. "I take all my style cues from Crystal and Sugar."

munching until he'd chewed a hole through the chocolate egg. We distracted him with a baby carrot while the Peeps family scampered to safety."

"We're in fine spirits," said George Peeps. "Dominic's sharp teeth saved the day."

At Crystal Peeps's insis-tence, all charges against Dominic have been dropped. "I wouldn't dream of pressing charges," said Crystal Peeps. "I love Dominic! Believe me, you can't buy this kind of pub-licity. I've got him scheduled for *Sweet Nothings* next week. George is designing a won-derful hutch, and Brian has drawn up a food pyramid for Dominic's edification. Best of all, Sugar has asked him to es-cort her to the Peeple's Choice Awards next week. He's dan-gerous company, but in any case we'll get our pictures in *Peeple* magazine."

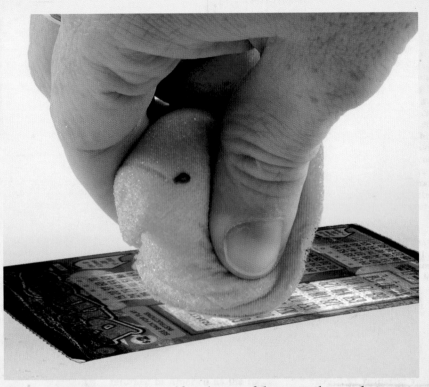

Lotto madness: Bebe McKor perfects her scandalous scratching technique.

Untrustworthy trio: Dr. Roberts and the McKors show no remorse.

In related news, three Peepsville residents were arrested yesterday on charges of fraud and embezzlement. "Dr. Rosebud Roberts didn't even try to build the Chocolaser 3000," said Detective Larry "Pop" Sicle, who apprehended the research scientist at the gorgeous ranch-style home of Bebe and Kevin McKor. "I followed up on a hot tip from Hazel Dugan, a cellophane-wrapped hard candy," he said. "She's been keeping tabs on the human population of Peepsville."

Detective Sicle found the trio sitting around the kitchen table, frantically scratching off lottery tickets. "They shot the whole wad on scratch 'n' match games," he said. "I saw Bebe McKor using Little Columbus as her scratching tool."

"I can't wait for the trial," said Crystal Peeps. "Those folks are absolutely shameless."

9 a.m.: Sunday morning. Pops is unwinding with his favorite h[o]
Easy on the cornflakes, Sweetie!

Where do Peeps come from, Mommy?

beverage. Puffy Sue likes cornflakes with her sugar.

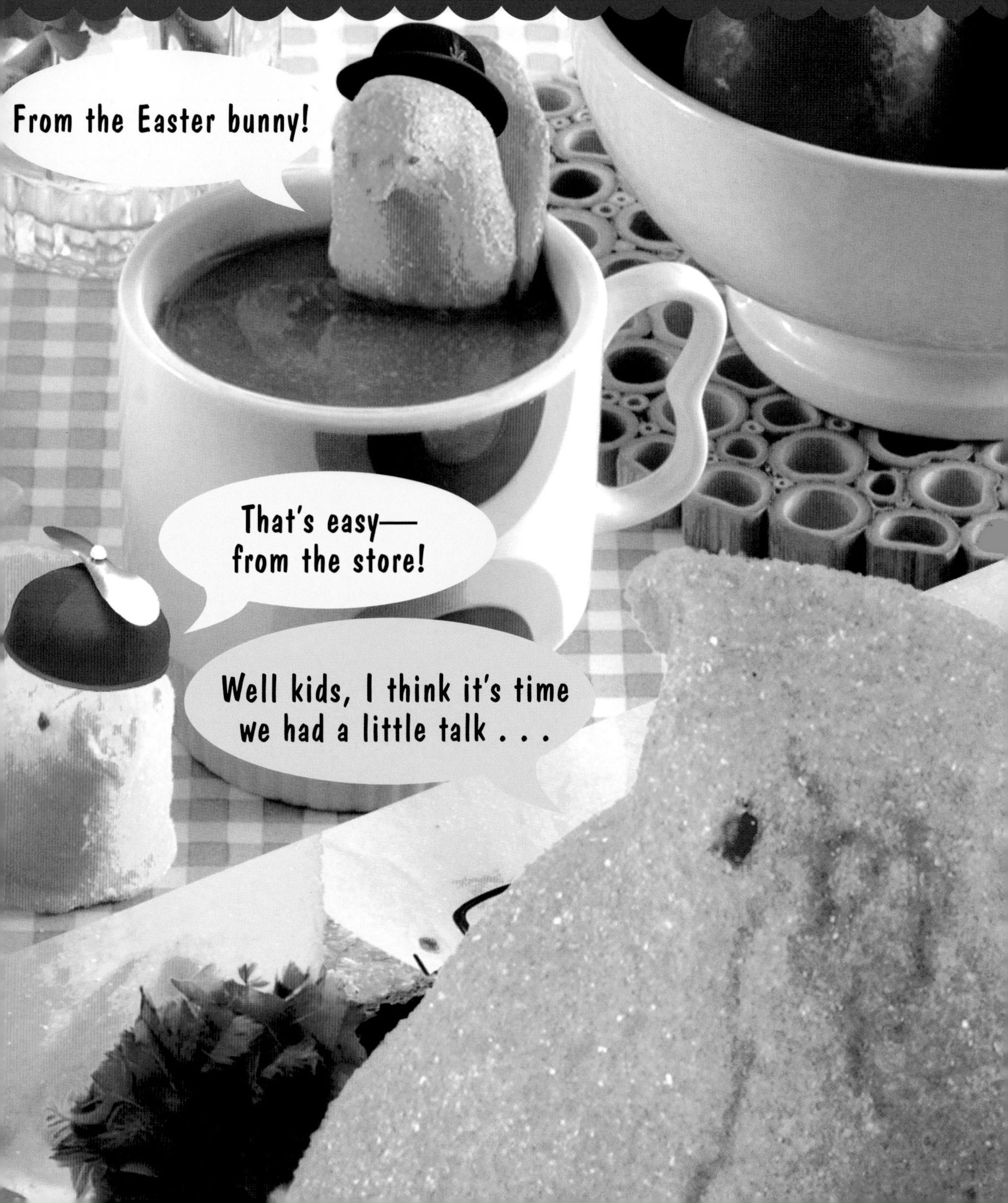

Your father and I
met at Just Born
way back when...

JUST BORN PEEPS TRUE FACTS

Marshmallow Peeps were first developed by the Rodda Candy Company of Lancaster, Pennsylvania. Each Peeps chick was hand-squeezed through a pastry tube. They looked like the lovely Rodda Sisters, whose photograph appears on page 71.

In 1953, Just Born, Inc., of Bethlehem, Pennsylvania, acquired the Rodda Candy Company.

In 1954, Just Born mechanized the Marshmallow Peeps–forming process. Here are some archival photographs of Just Born employees tending to new Peeps.

Just Born is now one of the world's largest manufacturers of novelty marshmallow candy. Dedicated workers produce as many as 4.2 million Marshmallow Peeps each day and over one billion Marshmallow Peeps each year.

It takes six minutes to create one Marshmallow Peep.

Leona Connors, Margaret Laurence, Caroline Bennet, and Anna Holiack

Delores Pender

Peeps Chicks and Bunnies come in five colors: yellow, pink, lavender, blue, and white. Yellow Chicks are the most popular.

One Peep has 32 calories and zero grams of fat.

Marshmallow Peeps are the top-selling non-chocolate Easter candy, jelly beans included.

Just Born estimates that over 700 million Marshmallow Peeps Chicks and Bunnies are consumed each Easter. How many will you eat?

A vintage Rodda Peeps advertisement, circa 1950

Mary Colli, May Destch, Rosie Torres, Janice Bohing, and Anna Sandor

Ann Fuko decorating Peeps

Marshmallow Peeps aren't just for snacking. Why not try the crafts and recipes in Dr. Rosebud Roberts's scrapbook on pages 20–25? You will find other great ideas at www.marshmallowpeeps.com.

The Peepsquatch is an urban legend, but Just Born once created a Marshmallow Peeps Bunny covered in toasted coconut. Its disappearance is shrouded in mystery!

"Sweets to the sweet: farewell!"

— *William Shakespeare*

THE AUTHORS

FOR HILLARY

ACKNOWLEDGMENTS

The authors would like to thank Matt Pye of Just Born, Inc. Special thanks to Gail Anderson, David Atkin, Darren Cox, Caroline Hannah, Susan Homer, Owain Hughes, Arlene Kahn, Ahmer Khan, Lisa Marks. Starring Hillary Kahn as Dr. Rosebud Roberts, Helen Kor as Bebe McKor, and Christopher "Silk" Johnson as Kevin McKor. Aaliytha Davis is the gleeful victim of a Peeps avalanche! Blankie Egg's wardrobe provided by Miss Olivia Chiossone.

Editor: Howard Reeves
Production Manager: Kaija Markoe

Library of Congress Cataloging-in-Publication Data

Masyga, Mark.
Peeps : a candy-coated tale / by Mark Masyga and Martin Ohlin.
p. cm.
1. Peeps (Trademark)—Humor. I. Ohlin, Martin. II. Title.

PN6231.P334M37 2006
813'.6—dc22
2005027829
ISBN 0-8109-5995-X

Printed and bound in China
10 9 8 7 6 5 4 3 2 1

harry n. abrams, inc.
a subsidiary of La Martinière Groupe
115 West 18th Street
New York, NY 10011
www.hnabooks.com

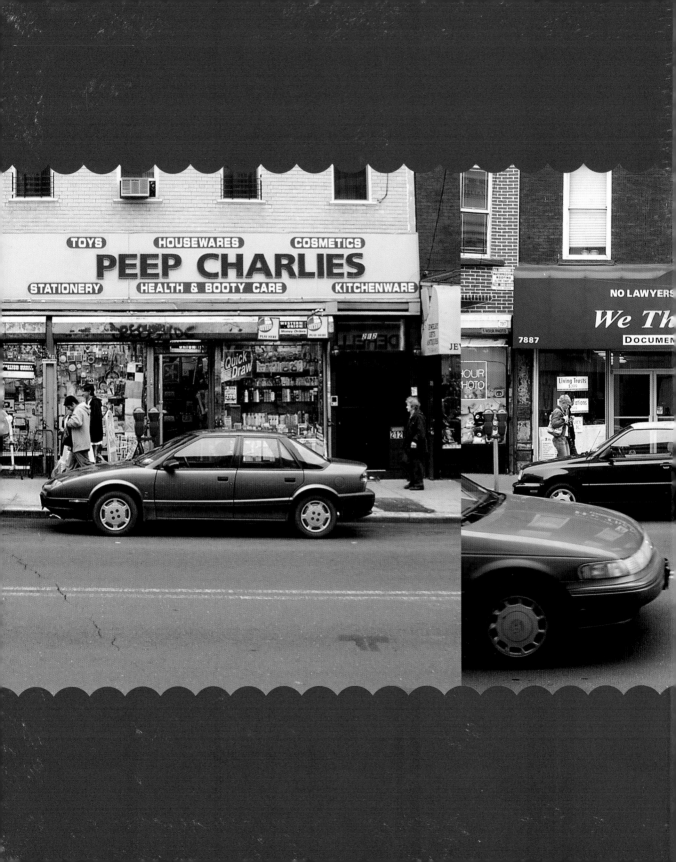